Adv⸺ ⸺⸺⸺

This is a must read for the masses. In over 25 years I've rarely seen a more common sense approach to understanding and combating the many economic issues facing Americans. This book is the place to start! Jay puts his perspective into a tool that needs to be in your box.
David Decker CMFC, CRPC, AAMS

This is a great resource for anyone who finds himself or herself wandering through the maze that they have come to know as their financial "picture". First steps and small attainable goals are important; this quick read is a great first step that seems manageable and not too "farfetched".
Father Mike Besson
Rector of St. John's
La Porte, Texas

You'll find almost every mistake you could possibly make in this book.... now YOU don't have to make them!! Jay's book offers an insider's look at finances in easy to understand stories that really hit home. No one is better qualified to help you row upstream in today's rocky waters than Jay Meador. Finally, an easy way to understand the financial world - just in time...
Debbie Davis
The Debbie Davis Show
Dallas, Texas

Is There Hope For Me?

By

Jay Meador, CFP®

Lessons Learned Publishing
Bryan, Texas

CFP® and Certified Financial Planner™ are trademarks of Certified Financial Planner Board of Standards, Inc.

This book is a work of non-fiction. Unless otherwise noted, the author and the publisher make no explicit guarantees as to the accuracy of the information contained in this book and in some cases, names of people and places have been altered to protect their privacy.

Further Disclaimer: The information contained in this book does not purport to be a complete description of the securities markets, or developments referred to in this material. Any information is not a complete summary or statement of all available data necessary for making an investment decision and does not constitute a recommendation. Any opinions are those of the author and not necessarily those of RJFS or Raymond James. Expressions of opinion are as of the initial book publishing date and are subject to change without notice. Recommendations, specific investments or strategies discussed may not be suitable for all investors. Past performance may not be indicative of future results. Raymond James Financial Services, Inc. is not responsible for the consequences of any particular transaction or investment decision based on the content of this book. You should discuss any tax or legal matters with the appropriate professional.

ISBN-13: 978-0-9822547-0-7   ISBN-10: 0-9822547-0-9
Cover design by adWhite (www.adWhite.com)
Printed in the United States of America

Acknowledgments

...no one mind is complete by itself. All truly great minds have been reinforced through contact with other minds. Every mind needs association and contact with other minds in order to grow and expand – Dr. Napoleon Hill

When one writes a collection of stories, it is commonly understood that the thank you list will be a long one. This book is no exception.

First, thank you to Bob Allen, my old branch manager at A. G. Edwards for having enough faith in me to hire me. Bob, you were a guide and support for me during some very dark times.

David Decker, thank you for your friendship, constant guidance and support.

Robert C. and Peggy Ford for the examples of determination and will power that they have been for me.

Steve Simmons for the use of your story in hopes that it would inspire hope in others.

My father Curt Meador, who helped me develop an entrepreneurial spirit which has helped me write this book.

Debbie Oaks, for all you've done through the years and in my life as support on this and many, many other projects that we have accomplished together. Patty Thompson for your input and help.

Russ Ford, my cousin and best friend who is always there when I need him.

Joy and John Hall for their story, their love, and their constant support.

Karen, my wife, who is my rock and my biggest inspiration.

Dr. Kozhi Sidney Makai, who guided me through this whole process

Bryan Mayberry – thanks for the wonderful cover concept. It is perfect.

Thank you to Chris Peterson, my friend and attorney, who helped with the Estate section.

My grandfather, Robert Ford, whose memory I will always cherish.

And finally, my mother Carol Ford, who has been the greatest mother, mentor, example, and friend that a son could ask for. If all mothers were like you, this world would be a much better place.

Contents

Introduction

Some of my fondest memories growing up are of the times I spent with my Grandfather. He was my first male mentor. Retired at an early age, he made lots of time for his grandkids. He took us fishing, hunting, and most importantly, he taught us how to pray. He was my inspiration to read the Bible from cover to cover when I was only twelve. It was easy to admire how smart he was, though he never even finished the 6th grade. Yet, coming from the poorest of families, he amassed considerable wealth.

How did he do it? That is the purpose for this book. It is the simplest, yet seemingly most elusive of philosophies; most of us don't get it until much later in life. Fortunately, as long as you have income, it is never too late to start managing your money better and change the course of your financial future.

Despite his tutelage, I had to learn the hard way how simple his philosophy was. Shortly after graduating from Texas A&M University with a Bachelor of Arts degree, I started my own business in retail sales distribution. Being bright, hard working, and enjoying what I did helped me to be successful for many years. Having my wife as my business partner helped us make a lot of money, especially so as she was the organized one.

Our business expanded and thrived for the better part of ten years, until I grew tired of the whole thing. As with all things with which one loses interest, we started to decline at a steady and rapid pace. Although my income had dwindled, I maintained the standard of living I had grown comfortable in, making a common, yet financially deadly error: I started relying on credit to pull me through where my regular income had fallen short of my needs.

In January of 1998, I walked into the local A. G. Edwards office. Not only was I buried in debt; I had virtually nothing to show for all our success and hard work. Fortunately, the branch manager knew of me by reputation as well as my past success and decided to take a chance on me. In May of 1998 I had passed the Series 7, the basic stockbroker's test, along with the company training program. It was official: I was a stockbroker for A.G. Edwards!

In August of the following year, I was beginning to wonder if my branch manager and I had both made a big mistake. The market was dropping and most of the wonderful stocks that I had gotten my clients into were losing money. People were not happy with me, and I wasn't happy with myself. I knew that if I was going to continue to be a stockbroker, I had to do a better job of learning my trade, and get more education.

So I started taking online courses at the College for Financial Planning. I was determined to become a Certified Financial Planner™, CFP®. Upon reflection, that one decision saved my career. After the events that took place on September 11th 2001, being enrolled in the program was the only thing that kept me from leaving this business too.

By now you're probably wondering what all this has to do with my grandfather, and what made him a success. Simply put, had I really listened to my grandfather's sage advice, I could have avoided a lot of pain, debt and a 'hard-knocks' education. His words:

"SPEND LESS THAN YOU MAKE,
WISELY SAVE AND INVEST THE DIFFERENCE
OVER A LONG PERIOD OF TIME."

There are two very important things that I have learned during my studies: Firstly, the knowledge I now have had brought me back to that very simple phrase and secondly, I realized that I was not alone. I was not the only person in the world that needed help following this very simple, yet golden, concept. It is with this in mind that I write this book in dedication to my grandfather, Robert Ford.

1

Spend Less Than You Make.
Your Budget is the Solid Foundation to Build On.

In 1965 my parents divorced. My father didn't contribute much in the way of child support, so my mother set to the task of raising her three children on a lab technician's salary. She did not ask for my grandfather's financial help, and none was given. He had made it through his hard times, now it was my mother's time to see what she was made of. Mom had already been trained in how to deal with money problems. Giving her financial help would not have helped her in the long run, nor would it have made her stronger.

We kept our two-story house, and Mom immediately found a sitter that would exchange some of her services for room and board, as my two sisters and I were all young at the time. She then worked out a budget that any financial planner would have been proud to call their own.

Because each budget should be personally tailored to each individual's circumstances, I am not going to go into the specifics of budget planning. That needs to be done one-on-one with your partner or financial advisor. However, with my mother's permission, I will tell you how and why she arranged her budget. This is based on her take home or net (after payroll deductions) pay. You will figure your budget the same way, on your net income.

Item #1 Pay God the first 10%. Beginning with my great grandmother, my family has always given 10% of our income to our church or other faith-based charity. Her motto – put God first and He will help you with the rest."

Item #2 Pay yourself 10% every month, just like you're paying a bill. As the first thing, my mother needed a car, so she borrowed the money from the credit union and paid the car off in two years. She continued to drive that same car for several years, *and* she continued to make payments to the credit union just as if she still owed money on the car. Only these payments went into her savings account and not the credit union's loan repayment department.

This strategy built her savings account steadily and in a reasonable amount of time. After that, she would move excess money over to an investment account she started with the money she had saved. Many years later, when she needed a new car, (she had driven hers as far as it would go), she had the cash to pay for it; she continued to pay her savings account the car payment as she had been doing. My mother often told me, "Some people look for things to spend money on when they get something paid off. I use my money for what I need, but I want my money to work for me, so I only borrow money for the things that I absolutely need like housing and transportation. The rest of it can wait; I'll pay cash, or do without." It was a very wise way to live.

<u>Item #3 Pay your house payment, commit no more than 30% of your income to it.</u> Your home is a very good investment, and the largest single piece of most people's investment portfolio. Unfortunately too many people today buy much more home than they can afford. When we were old enough for my sister to be the sitter, my mother sold our house and we moved to an apartment. The house was too much for a working mom to keep up with; apartment living was cheaper, and provided us with amenities like a swimming pool.

My mother understood the value of owning some real estate as an investment, so she bought a piece of property as soon as she could. Another piece of wisdom she would often share with us was, "Never own something that owns you. If it costs more to keep up and pay for than you can afford, it will emotionally own you."

<u>Item #4 Use no more than 30% of your monthly income for utilities, food, insurance, gas and other bills.</u> She would say, "If you're paying more than 30% on bills and needs, you are probably spending money on things that you don't really need. Are you buying new or used? Can you walk instead of drive? Do you really need to go at all? Do you conserve electricity? Do you buy the bargain brand foods or the name brands? Where do you shop? Can you do it yourself instead of paying to have it done?" All very good questions we need to be asking ourselves as a part of our daily financial discipline.

It's important to remember that my mother was raised to not have debt except for a house or a car, so she never paid credit card debt. Credit card debt is probably responsible for more people *not* being able to realize their financial goals and dreams than any other single area of borrowing.

<u>Item #5 Pay an emergency fund 10% a month.</u> I can't remember a single time (other than her first car) that my mother was ever forced to borrow money to pay for an unexpected event. She taught my sisters and I that, "emergencies happen, preplan for them."

<u>Item #6 Pay for fun with cash now or save for more fun later at 10% a month.</u> I could spend an entire chapter on this one item. I have certainly been guilty of spending too much money on entertainment and, like so many people today, I charged it now and paid a premium for it later. My mother would say, "Time invested is better than money spent."

She read to, and with, us. We learned to play all kinds of card, and inexpensive board, games. The only time we ate out was Friday nights. We went to a fast food hamburger restaurant, or once a month when she got paid we went to a real restaurant instead of a fast food restaurant.

If we wanted to go on a family vacation, she would pay us for doing things around the house and then she would match dollar-for-dollar the money that we put into "THE VACATION JAR." When the jar was full she would deposit the money into an interest-bearing account. We would fill it again and again until we had enough money to go on the trip that we had planned. Sometimes it would take us two years or more to save for a real vacation, but it was always paid for before we went. We stayed with friends and family wherever we could, or stayed at lower priced places to cut costs. We took some great family vacations!

Item #7 If your budget gets out of line, find a way to make extra money until you get it back in line. My mother groomed dogs on the side for a while to supplement our income so she could meet our needs. She was adamant that we should always "make it, don't borrow it."

It's funny, but looking back from today's standards most people would say that we were poor. I didn't feel that way then, and still don't today. We always had what we needed. And most of all, we had a mother that loved and spent time with us. She didn't try to buy our affection through throwing money or gifts at us; she didn't give us what we wanted, but she certainly gave us what we needed. Learning that we had to earn what we wanted was a loving lesson taught that caused us to be stronger.

Save Wisely and Invest the Difference:
Specific goals and a little qualified help go a long way.

Talk about a loser; that was John. He had long hair and wasn't going to college. Even worse, he wanted to marry my sister, Joy. The fact that he would never amount to anything wasn't bad enough; he was stealing my cook! Now I would have to do the cooking for the family. A fate far worse than death itself!

Sure, he was a likeable enough guy, but he certainly wasn't brother-in-law material. Joy was smart and going to be a very successful teacher. This guy was going to be a pipe fitter. What was she thinking? And I hate cooking!

John did have some good traits though. Besides being likable, he was a hard worker, wasn't too proud to ask for advice, and (most of all) his father had taught him how to budget as well as set specific goals.

John knew he wanted to have his new truck paid off before he married Joy, so he set up a specific time frame and schedule. By following his goal, he was able to accomplish just that in the time frame he had set for himself.

John also knew that he wanted to be in a home instead of an apartment when he and Joy got married. They sat down together and worked out a plan to get themselves in a home they could afford as soon as possible.

Because it was just the two of them, both Joy and John worked and watched their budget. They were in a home they could afford in a short period of time. John had no problem working overtime, and that was a plus which had helped them reach their goal that much sooner.

Then there was that whole not-being-too-proud to get help thing. My uncle, Robert Ford's son (also Robert) was a financial advisor; John and Joy went to see him. They already knew what they wanted to achieve financially, and they knew the specific time frame that they wanted it in. Step one was the easy part.

My uncle told Joy and John that it was obvious that they already understood the importance of saving, (putting money into short term interest-bearing accounts for a specific, future purchase). John had also been contributing to his 401(k) plan at work, not because he was such a great investor, but because they matched up to 5%. Even the super-dummy wouldn't let free money get away!

Soon John was changing jobs and wanted to know what to do with the money. At thirty-two, most people his age would have pulled that money out and spent it. But my uncle advised him to roll it into an Individual Retirement Account (IRA) with a conservative mutual fund, which John did. Then he got my uncle to review his plan and help him set the account up according to his retirement goals.

Over the years as Joy or John got raises, instead of running out and buying something, they would increase their savings or add to their investment portfolio. In a relatively short period of time, they had everything their family needed for their two kids (a boy and a girl, also planned) so they were able to start working on getting those things that they wanted without disturbing their long-term retirement goals.

In 1986, my business brought in more money than Joy and John made *combined*. I was going to retire long before that idiot brother-in-law (you know, the one who stole my cook?). Today, yearly interest and gains alone from their portfolio amount to more than I make in five months of work. Years ago John told me that he would retire comfortably at or before age 65. My mother told me that if Joy and John said they were going to have a male child at 2:00 on a certain day, she would just show up because she knew it would happen exactly that way. They had a goal and a persistent purpose. I had a goal without persistence or purpose. I'm reminded of the "Tortoise and the Hare" story at this point.

John is on track to retire much sooner than I am. They do what they want, when they want to without worrying about the cost. There are only two things I gained from all this: Now, I'm actually a good cook (if you don't mind it smoky), and the knowledge that my 'idiot' brother-in-law may actually be a genius.

<u>Over a Long Period of Time:</u>
What is your definition of long time?

In 1972 I was twelve years old and had managed to save a whopping $400 in my savings account. I decided that I wanted to invest $200 of it in stock, so I got with my granddad and he and I bought some shares in one stock that he had been closely following After two years, the stock had doubled in value and I sold my shares. One hundred percent profit, what a thrill!

In 1987 I was riding around with my granddad and we were talking about old times.

I said, "Hey Pa, you remember that stock that you helped me buy when I was twelve and I doubled my money in just two years?"

"Yes I do, you did well with that stock," he said.

"How much money did you invest in it?" I asked.
"$5,000", he said.

"So how much did you make when you sold yours?" I asked.

"I haven't sold mine yet but it's worth about $100,000 today."

OK, you do the math: if his $5,000 was worth $100,000 then my $200 would have been worth $4,000. To this day I can't remember why I sold that stock.

Maybe I had decided to sell when I doubled my money. Maybe I needed to buy something. Maybe I listened to someone who told me that I should sell it, after all, the stock and the market might go down and who would want to take a chance of losing all that money? Regardless of the reason, I learned something valuable that day. My definition of a long time at 14 years old was much different than my granddad's definition of it. How many of us have a 14 year old's definition of a long time? Now to my defense, I didn't have what you would call a well rounded or balanced portfolio.

Owning just one stock, no matter how secure it may seem has a large degree of risk to it no matter how sophisticated your investment person may be. My grandfather had a very well balanced portfolio and enjoyed taking very good care of it doing careful research and following each position daily like a job. He could have absorbed the downturn of one stock in his portfolio without much grief, but I couldn't. But how many of us have treated a well balanced mutual fund as if it were an individual stock, and sold it just because we were afraid of a down turn in the market or we just wanted to spend the money on something that we wanted? In my experience, many investors only hold an investment for an average of 2 years. Although history is no guarantee of future success, it has shown us that markets do come back and that true long term well balanced investing can pay off. My granddad was certainly proof of that for me.

Spend or save; have goals or have it now;
trade or invest; emotion or DISCIPLINE?

There is a commercial on TV that part of the catch phrase is "I want it all, I want it now." That may be fine for whatever product they are selling, but the inherent problem is that too many people are starting to use that same philosophy to run their lives. It is a philosophy that not only can have long term bad effects for an individual, but if too many people really start to live their lives that way, it can have terrible long term effects on our country. Look at the housing market crunch as an example. We allowed too many people to have homes that they wanted now instead of working with them and teaching them how to properly budget and save for a home later when they could handle the payments. Now we are in the worst mortgage crunch that we have seen in my lifetime.

As a child I watched a black and white TV for years after all my friends had color TV. If I wanted to do something fun like go to a movie or an amusement park, I earned the money to do it. My mother wanted to do two things with us, the first was to teach us to earn our own way, the second was to make sure that the time she did spend with us was as free of emotional baggage as possible, i.e., thinking about bills. I'm proud to say that she accomplished both fairly well.

Joy and John gave up things they wanted early on in life in order to get almost everything they wanted later and not have the baggage of debt, or having to work longer, associated with it. And because they were smart enough to know that they didn't know about investments, they got qualified advice to help them reach their goals.

When I started with A. G. Edwards, my granddad opened a trading account with them. I also opened one for myself. A trading account is an account set up for short term trades. We had a great time picking stocks on a short term basis. Keep in mind that this was not his real money. Real money is any money that has a purpose; this was his play money or his gambling money...it was extra money that had no real purpose. His real money was in his investment account. Also keep in mind that before he ever became a trader he was an investor, this made him a much better trader, plus he had the money to risk if things went wrong. I am sure that one of the reasons he set up the account was to help me get some real world experience in short term trading, but what neither one of us thought about at the time was that he had paid his dues as an investor and I hadn't. After he passed away and wasn't around to help me, I realized that I wasn't the trader I thought I was, and what's worse is, I didn't have the money to lose if things went wrong like he did. My decisions became mostly emotional instead of disciplined and I ended up losing money.

Needless to say, I don't do much trading anymore. Perhaps someday I will again, after I've paid my dues. Fear and greed may seem to rule the market at times, but emotions shouldn't rule the way you handle your money. Bottom-line, if you don't set goals, have a budget, save, invest, and look past the short term, you will probably have some major difficulties down the road. That's not to say that you won't have them anyway, but as my mother says "emergencies happen, plan for them." So start planning now: "Spend less than you make and wisely save and invest the difference over a long period of time."

2

Help! I've committed financial suicide and it may be too late for me.

"Life after death"

Steve was living a great life. He was single, had a well paying job, and lots of good time buddies to hang out with. His father was a banker, so Steve did understand a little about saving and the value of having a retirement plan through work. Self admittedly, he had never really asked his father for money advice nor listened much when it was given, after all he was single and his only real goal was to live life to it's fullest today. That went fine for a while, Steve had some savings and his retirement plan at work was growing fine until Steve got his first DWI. For some people that would have been a wakeup call, but not Steve, by this point he was addicted to drinking and didn't want to admit it. So, he did what any good alcoholic would do and paid the massive amount of money to fix the DWI, but ignored the real problem, and continued his same lifestyle.

Without going into a lot of details I'm sure you have figured out where this is heading. A few years later, Steve has picked up two more DWIs, he's in deep debt, and he's about to lose his job. In Texas three

DWIs and you go to prison. Steve had hit rock bottom. He called my cousin Russ and asked him for money. Fortunately for Steve, Russ and I shared the same granddad, Robert Ford. In other words, Russ was willing to help Steve but not with money, Russ would only help Steve with his real needs first. Russ's dad Robert, the investment guy that helped my brother in law John, suggested to Russ that he tell Steve he would only support him through his Church and that Steve had to go see the church pastor for advice and help. Steve, having no other real options, went.

Matt, the pastor at Russ's church, had several sessions with Steve. They talked about everything from hunting and fishing to faith and trusting in God. At the end of the third session with Steven, after Matt was convinced that Steve was truly ready and able to receive help, Matt gave the authorization to pay some of Steve's immediate bills directly to the companies that Steve owed the money to. Steve had signed up for a rehab program, but there were still complications regarding his third DWI, so he went to the courthouse to check on the time frame of the trial against the time frame for rehab. At the courthouse Steve was informed that some critical evidence had been lost and the third DWI case had been dropped. Steve, seeing this as a second chance from God, entered the rehab program almost immediately and with a much lighter heart.

When Steve came out of rehab five weeks later, he was a man on a mission to help others and serve God. But he was also a man that still had some serious debt. Matt continued to authorize payment of Steve's absolute necessities such as rent and truck payments for a short period until Steve started getting paid again, then Steve was on his own. He had to learn how to support himself within his budget. Steve started out by prioritizing his bills. Then he called everyone else that he owed, explained the situation, and made arrangements to start getting them paid.

It wasn't easy for Steve, especially at first. By the time he paid the bills he had promised to pay there was little left over for food. Steve learned to like Ramen noodles and peanut butter. He picked up extra work where he could or helped Russ when he could (payback for the money Russ had given to the church on his behalf). The rest of his free time was spent at AA meetings and serving God through helping others. Steve was barely getting by, but all of his needs were being met. Time and time again when Steve thought he was about to hit a major obstacle, something would open up and Steve would be just fine. Steve became a living example of how God will help you with needs if you trust Him. Steve also realized that he didn't get into this mess over night and that it was going to take years and discipline to get out of it.

Less than two years after accepting his problem and starting on a plan to recovery, Steve has above average credit, a small emergency fund, and is even looking at restarting his retirement plan contributions at work. He isn't adding on any new debt and is doing well at paying down what he has. He also has enough to eat out occasionally. Steve probably won't be able to retire at 65 or take elaborate vacations in his life, but with his current spending discipline, and a little guidance with future investments, Steve has a real good chance at being able to live out his later retirement years without too much worry about money and bills.

There are several morals to this story. The first is that Russ was smart enough not to give Steve money directly. That would have only caused more problems. Russ turned his money and Steve's problems over to someone that was qualified to help Steve. Then, Steve had to accept that he had a problem that was beyond his control and allow himself to be lead in a direction that would fix it. And finally, Steve had to do his part daily to keep his discipline, work ethic, and attitude on the right track. Steve will probably never have material wealth the way he used to perceive it, but he has come to experience a type of wealth that is greater than many people ever have a chance to have. He's happy again, he has learned how to handle obstacles without worry, and he looks beyond himself to the service of others. Steve has experienced the wealth of life after death.

Financial Suicide:
Fighting over Principle

"It's the principle of the thing." We've all heard that phrase. An attorney friend of mine once told me that those words were financial music to his ears. Basically, no matter what the cost, I want to win. Now, if the cause is great enough, I'm right there with you. Freedom, for example, I'm in. What ever it takes, that's worth fighting for. But let's look at what some people in a divorce situation spend thousands of dollars fighting for.

I heard of one case where the couple spent one hour fighting over who got a piece of property worth about $150. This was with both lawyers present. Two lawyers at $100 an hour each is $200. Time and time again people fight over a piece of property that is worth far less than the money they are spending to fight for it.

Then there are the situations where people automatically look for the biggest, meanest, and most expensive attorneys around to represent them. That approach is fine for some situations, but before you go hunting with a cannon, make sure you're hunting something bigger than a rabbit. You'll kill the rabbit, but there won't be anything left.

In 1989, when I owned my own retail sales business, I got a call from some copy toner salesman that said he was calling to confirm our order for toner. My wife was not in the office; she did all that stuff, so I gave him the information and went on my way. When the order came in she asked what it was and I said, "It's the copy toner that you ordered." I felt like a fool when she explained to me that I had been had. The first thing I did was call Mike, our attorney. I wanted to sue the company, and I didn't care what it cost. Mike, being an honest attorney, (yes they do exist) convinced me that a much better use of my time and money would be to simply return the toner, contact the Better Business Bureau, and focus my time and energies on my business.

In the early 1970's my uncle, Robert C. Ford, went to battle with a mayor in a small Texas town. The individual was not only the mayor, but he owned the water works, he was the distict attorney, the town judge, and the chief of the fire department. After many years and thousands of dollars of his personal money spent, my uncle was directly responsible for getting the mayor impeached. It was the first time in the history of Texas that a mayor had been impeached. I have always been very proud of him and my aunt for standing up against something that they considered to be very wrong, despite the personal cost.

Yes, principles are great to have, and sometimes worth fighting for, but before you go to battle for one, step back and ask yourself is it truly a principle that you are fighting for, or is it an emotion? And is there another way to get what you want without a full fledged fight? Legal cost can ruin a portfolio for a long period of time. Look at it this way; is the principle you're fighting for worth you working an additional ten years, or cutting your budget by another 20 to 30 percent or more? If so, go for it.

Financial Suicide
Lottery Mentality

Wouldn't you love to win the lottery? What would you do with the money? How would you spend your time? I could spend hours thinking about that. And that's part of the problem. Some people actually list their retirement plan as winning the lottery or waiting for some big inheritance that may or may not come.

As I mentioned in the introduction of this book, there was a time in my life that I was making far less money than I was spending and yet I didn't slow down on my spending habits. I refer to this as the "lottery mentality." Before the lottery came into being in Texas, it was Ed McMahon. He was going to bring me my sweepstakes winnings or, business was going to miraculously increase without my doing anything to make it happen. Needless to say, that plan wasn't working very well. Then I woke up and decided that I had lost my passion for what I was doing and that's why I was daydreaming instead of working. I had at least taken step one. But my spending habits still had to change and unfortunately that didn't happen until I became a CFP®.

I've seen people, myself included, take money from retirement accounts, pay taxes and penalties, and use the money to pay down debt. But then turn right around and build up more debt. It's as if we think we are going to receive this big paycheck from heaven, so it doesn't matter how we spend money today. In my experience that philosophy doesn't pay off as much as we would like it to. More often, we wind up depressed and in deeper debt.

I heard of one couple that spent thousands and thousands of dollars on their daughter's wedding, then one year later the marriage ended in divorce, the main reason, money problems. Now it's certainly nice to give your daughter a big wedding if that's what everyone wants, but wouldn't it be better to give her a specific amount of money up front and say, "this is for your wedding, if you over spend the rest comes from you, if you under spend you keep the difference.
The couple will learn a lot about budgeting and hopefully working together on a joint goal.

Most sales happen because of emotion, not logic. If you have a budget that you are sticking to, you are less likely to let yourself get carried away by a feeling.

People buy because it feels right. That's ok if you can pay cash for it, and all of your other goals are on track, but if you can't, you better take some advice from my mother and either wait until you can pay cash and have all your other goals on track, or decide you don't need it after all. This whole thing has sure been a lesson to me.

3

Back on Track
Part I: The Mission Statement

My friend Rodger once told me "Not having a mission statement can be dangerous. It's as if you spend a good deal of your life climbing a ladder, only to get to the top and finding that all along your ladder has been leaning against the wrong wall." Unfortunately, I got this advice at a time that I was on top of a ladder against the wrong wall.

The mission statement is the first step to getting your life and finances on track. It describes who you are and what you're about. In 1995 I had achieved a level of success in my business that only about 5% of the people in it had ever achieved, and yet I was unhappy. I had succeeded in raising my level of spending above my income, I was having marital problems and my business was starting to suffer. I felt as though everyday was a daily grind. Then one Sunday as I sat in church, my priest and friend Mark Crawford told this story. He explained that it was not from the Bible but it made such an impact on me that I had to share it with you.

Jesus, John, and Peter were at the edge of a mountain and getting ready to walk up it. Jesus looked at both disciples and said "pick up a stone." John, being the evangelist, picked up the largest stone he could find. Peter, being a bit more practical, picked up a small rock. When they reached the top of the mountain, Jesus turned both the stones into bread. John having the large stone had a very large loaf of bread. Peter got a very small piece of bread. As they were getting ready to go down the mountain, Jesus once again said "pick up a stone." This time Peter grabbed the largest stone he could find, and John picked up a tiny pebble. At the bottom of the mountain, they all came to a lake. Jesus said "now cast your stones into the lake". John threw his pebble into the lake as Peter's stone plopped into the water. For a moment Peter looked at his stone as if expecting something to happen to it, and then he looked up at Jesus. Jesus simply looked at Peter and said "for whom were you carrying the stone?"

All at once I realized; I was Peter. My main focus was me, my wants, and my needs. Oh sure I cared about others, my family, friends, and the church. But my real concern was my daily bread and I was so wrapped up in getting it so that I could continue to have the lifestyle that I wanted, that I had ended up with my ladder on the wrong wall. Now I'm not about to try to make you believe that everything was great for me after that sermon, on the contrary, it was simply a first step to a very long and hard road which included a career change, lots of education, frequent backsliding, and regular self examination. But I did get my mission statement that day; Serve God and others first and foremost.

I'm not going to begin to tell you how you should find your mission statement. Perhaps you will receive enlightenment from above as I did. Or, author Rick Warren has written a couple of books that I could recommend. However you do it, it's important to understand, that until you know who you are and what you are about, you shouldn't start climbing the ladder. Or at least look very carefully at the wall it's leaning up against.

Back on Track
Part II: The Big Picture

So after you know who you are and what you're about through your mission statement, then it's time to figure out what you want. What are your dreams? How will you achieve them? What sacrifices are you willing to make?

My friend and co-worker David Decker is the best I've ever known at seeing "The Big Picture." In other words, he knows what he wants for his future and he instinctively does the things that help him achieve it. I myself must be much more regimented about things. I have to set up a budget, write my goals down, and constantly reevaluate myself in order to reach my dreams. I'm sure being naturally lazy has something to do with it. David, on the other hand, seems to stay guided in the right direction and focused most of the time. He is at a point in life where he gets what he wants, does what he wants, and always pays for it out right. He claims that it's a product of a made up mind. Whatever it is, it's like watching a child solve a math problem without having to work the equation.

David says he simply pictures in his mind his one, five, ten, and twenty year goals. Then he does the things daily that help him achieve those goals. Now keep in mind, he's very specific about his goals, and he's not ridiculous about them. As he says, there are some things that would be nice to have but they aren't worth the sacrifice. Many people that I have met have a hard time visualizing a clear picture for themselves. If you ask them what their twenty year goal is they tell you something like "to be rich." Well I'm sorry but that's not a clear enough vision even for them. First, everyone has their own definition of "rich" so without a clear understanding of what your definition is you go nowhere. Second, why do you want to be rich? It's usually in answering the why question that we really start to see our real goals.

Once I had established that my mission in life was to serve others, I decided that I could serve them better as a financial planner, and that would be a way to meet my other goals as well. Then I realized that I work best with mainly female investors that have $200,000 in investable assets, so that was the market I decided to focus on. I also felt as though I could effectively serve about 200 clients a year without tearing into the other service aspects of work or my personal life. So after I had achieved my Certified Financial Planner™ designation I went to Raymond James where I set my own hours. I have set a five-year goal to have 200 clients that have more than $200,000 or more investable assets that I enjoy working with. The "that I enjoy working with" part is the most important thing to me. So even though the by-product of that may be more money, the priority is on helping people that want my help and that are easy to get along with. Also, I still have time to advise people that don't have money and write this book. Now that's something specific, and that's what I try to teach my clients to do.

This is just one of many goals. I have others that I have to make sure aren't conflicting with my main goals. The big picture is about seeing clearly the things that complete who you are, and then understanding the steps and compromises that you must take to achieve the dream. Notice that this time I used the word compromise instead of sacrifice. You see, if you really are doing what you feel called to do, it doesn't feel like a sacrifice. Sometimes I give up watching TV to do something with my family, help someone, or attend a meeting. But I am helping to complete my "Big Picture" when I do that, not making a sacrifice. When I give money to a worthy cause, take my puppet and read to kids, or cook for some charity, I am helping to add a piece to the jigsaw puzzle of my "Big Picture."

So start thinking now about what makes you happy and why it makes you happy, then decide if it builds you and others around you up or tears you down. Decide how you can make a positive difference in most of the things you do. Then start imagining how long it's going to take to achieve each of those things and make sure that they aren't in conflict with each other. Now you're on your way to defining your "Big Picture."

As I write this chapter, I realize that in some way I have written this book in reverse order, (somewhat like my life). You see, my mother knew what her mission statement was, "to be a great mom and provider." She also had the big picture and her other dreams and goals in place, so building a budget around all that and sticking to it was easy. She could see her daily motivation. Most people don't stick to their budgets because they can't see the daily motivation for it. That's where goals come into play.

Now that you hopefully have a mission statement and you have some clear pictures in your mind of what you want your future to look like and why, it's time to do the work of deciding what you are going to do daily, weekly, monthly, and yearly to reach those dreams. Husbands, be sure and include your wives in this, all the previous processes, and the ones to follow, trust me on this one, big mistake not to. Also if one of your goals is to be a better spouse, and it should be, then you should set some time aside daily for your spouse, even if it's a long phone conversation or letter. Communication with the important people in your life is a key component to making your goals work.

Next, establish a time horizon – that is, when you expect your goal to be complete – for each of your goals and investments. As a financial planner, it's important for me to say here that your investments should match your goals and time horizons. For example, if you're in your thirties and thinking that you might want to start your own business in ten years, it's probably not wise to put most of your investment dollars into your retirement account. Also match your risk tolerance to your investments and time horizon. For example, investing in growth stocks could require a ten year time horizon for suitable results. Look at your money as being in different jars that you are depositing funds into every month. Each jar has a specific purpose and time horizon. Each jar should be invested differently from the other jars. As you find yourself starting to realize some of your short term goals, you will be more motivated to stick to your budget.

Now comes the really hard part for me, the scheduling of my time. In my business it's easy to let my schedule direct me instead of me directing my schedule. I am constantly asking myself if what I am doing is moving me to or away from my goals. Understand, I'm not saying don't take some down time to relax and goof off, that's actually important from time to time, it's just that I have a tendency to over do the goof off part, so I have to schedule "goof off" time so I won't spend too much time doing it. Also, it's very important to say no from time to time when it comes to helping. I am a father, a husband, a grandfather, a member of a church, and three different organizations. I am constantly asked to do things for someone or some organization, so it's very important that I prioritize my time and not overbook so I can be at my best whenever I am doing something for others. I'm not going to show you my schedule or someone else's because you have to establish your schedule based on what's important to you, otherwise you won't stick to it. Just keep in mind that everything should relate back to whatever your mission statement is for yourself.

Lastly, schedule time to pray and meditate on your goals daily. The great athletes envision themselves going through successful motions constantly. If we can take time to envision the things that we are trying to accomplish and why we want to accomplish them, then ask a higher power than ourselves for help, it's amazing what can be achieved.

4

Things to Prepare For
Identity Theft

Clark had not received his credit card statement, so he called the company that issued it. "You've moved," they said. Clark had not moved, and so, it began. Clark was instructed to immediately contact Trans Union and tell them that he was a victim of identity theft. Trans Union contacted the other two credit bureaus to put a 12-year identity theft fraud alert on his account. One credit bureau was not very helpful. They kept asking for information before they would change the fraudulent address in Buffalo, N.Y. and they wanted a signed affidavit from his bank stating that he had been a victim of identity theft. But the biggest problem with the third bureau is that he never got to speak with a real person.

Clark had used that credit card recently to purchase something over the internet. Was that how the person got his personal information? No one knew for sure, but the thief had the last four digits of Clark's social security number, his password, and his credit card number. Clark went online to Google Earth and put in the address in Buffalo, NY that his address had been changed to. He was able to look directly at the apartment complex and find out who lived at the address. He contacted the local police, who contacted the Buffalo police. The Buffalo police seemed to be too busy to be bothered with it.

Clark felt as though his personal information had been sold to the thief by an insider. ABC news reported on August 5th, 2008 that organized crime hackers stole 41 million credit accounts recently. The thieves were using laptops near department stores with wireless software to hack into the information.

Then Clark went through the process of canceling everything that might have a problem associated with it. At this point he was justifiably nervous. When all was said and done, Clark had caught the problem before it had cost him anything except time and aggravation simply because he was aware of when his statements were due. How many of us are aware when our statements should show up every month?

I heard another story of a lady that had her purse stolen with all of her important information in it. Three months later she found out that a house had been purchased in her name. Most of the people I know either know someone that has been a victim of identity theft or have been a victim themselves, and yet the number of people that think they will become a victim is still relatively low. Jeff Foxworthy, this one's for you. *If you think your chances of winning the lottery are better than your chances of having your identity stolen, you might be a redneck*!

A few quick tips to avoid identity theft are: Never take your social security card with you. Memorize it, and leave it at home in a safe place. Carry only the credit or debit cards that you will need with you, leave the rest at home and in a safe place. Don't let your credit or debit card out of your sight. If you are paying at a restaurant follow the waiter to the cashier, or better yet, pay cash. Don't leave receipts behind if you are not paying cash. Shred any trash that contains personal information. Hide or lock up personal information at your home. Don't leave information in your computer unless you heavily protect it with passwords that you change often. When using passwords use at least 10 characters in your password and mix them up, (example. *JaY^)03)*M). Never give personal information to anyone that calls you or attempts to contact you on your computer. Finally, check your credit regularly. I am with a credit monitoring service that sends me emails if any activity happens with my credit. Don't be an identity theft redneck; be proactive in protecting your identity!

Things to Prepare For:
Estate Planning

You will die! Deal with it! If you own anything of value, you need some sort of estate plan. I am amazed by the number of people that don't have wills; it's as if they think nothing will happen to them so they don't need one.

My friend and attorney Chris Peterson has come up with a list of the 10 most common mistakes in estate planning. With his permission, I would like to share them with you:

#1 *Do nothing*: If you do nothing, the State decides for you. Administration becomes more difficult and costly.

#2 *Do it yourself*: The do it yourself kits are usually not state specific. This, once again, can result in a much more difficult and expensive probate.

#3 *Buying from a living trust salesman*: Living trusts are just one tool for estate planning. They aren't for everyone and in some states and circumstances they don't have any real advantages. Many are not properly drafted or funded. Despite what you are told by a living trust sales person, you will usually get much better advice and a better price if you use a licensed attorney to draft your will or trust.

#4 *Forgetting to update your will as things change in your life*: Many people create their first will after they have had kids. Unfortunately, it's also their last. This can also cost thousands of dollars to clean up.

#5 *Improper beneficiary designations*: Do yourself a favor: find a Certified Financial Planner™, load up copies of all your important documents and take them to his or her office. Tell them where you want everything to be when you die and get them to help you. The CFP® will cost less than most attorneys and for something like this, a CFP® is amply qualified to help.

#6 *Minor beneficiaries*: You have just forced the state to appoint a guardian for your child, and it will probably be someone like your ex-spouse or someone that doesn't know or care about your kids. If that's not good enough, the day your child turns 18 they are immediately entitled to every thing you left him or her at once, to spend however they choose.

#7 *Not updating a will when moving to a new state*: Probate may not be as easy.

#8 *Overlooking disability planning*: Have a durable and a medical power of attorney.

#9 *Improper estate planning with second marriage*: Community property rules, special retirement plan rules, provisions in the probate code, and the second spouse with the step children are just some of the things that need to be looked at.

#10 *Not choosing the right professionals to assist you*: Your attorney, CFP®, CPA, and insurance person are all part of the team working for you. Help them work together for your best interest. Pick an attorney that spends a great deal of their practice in estate planning. Pick a financial planner that will give you a holistic plan, not just sell you product.

I have many horror stories of people that died and left a mess for the people they loved to have to clean up just because they didn't take the time to plan or didn't know how to plan properly. Don't become one of those people, start working on your estate plan today.

<u>*Things to prepare for*</u>:
Emergencies/ Hard times

As I mentioned earlier in the book, my mother paid 10% of her income every month into an emergency fund. She always wanted to get enough in it so that she could move some of it into an investment fund, but I don't remember that ever happening. Raising three kids with only one income usually took care of that. The interesting thing is that she did have it when we needed it.

On September 11th, 2001 America was not prepared for the devastation and evil that came upon us. Whether it is from attack or natural disaster, there will always be things that come up that we are unprepared for, and yet if we are somewhat prepared isn't that better than nothing? Let's face it, some things are just in God's hands and there is nothing we can do about it. But what about the things we could handle but for what ever reason we simply never preplanned for them?

Health, life, disability, auto, home, and long term care insurance are just some of the ways that we can be a bit more prepared for emergencies. It seems like there is insurance for everything these days. Some is expensive and unnecessary. It's very important to find a planner that you trust to help you decide what is right for your needs.

But beyond all that, we have things like layoffs, deductibles on insurance, the car breaks down, a relative needs our help, or any number of things that can arise. How many of us have an emergency fund that would cover these things, or do we rely on credit, cashing in other funds, or someone else to pull us through? I am constantly asked how much should someone have in an emergency fund? My response is always to tell them that first we need to look closely at their individual situation and then decide what's right for them.

The Boy Scouts have the same motto that my mother has, "Be prepared." My mother has always said that it's easier to go into a hard situation if you're not agonizing over the cost. Perhaps the only real preparation we can have is to put back some emergency funds and review our insurance regularly. The final thing we can do is prepare like it's all up to us but pray like it's all up to God.

Things to Prepare For:
Keeping Fun in the Budget

"All work and no play," it can't be done long term and shouldn't be done, not if we are going to enjoy life at all. However, we also need to understand the balance of time and budget. From a money standpoint 10% of your take home pay after tax may not seem to be enough to have any fun, and for you single guys out there you are probably right. I don't know what to tell you dude except your goals need to be really big so that the sacrifice is worth it, or work more.

As far as the rest of you go, there are plenty of things to do that don't cost much money. The old pizza and a rental movie, a picnic, or some type of game come to mind. The main thing is that it is important to take some time to relax and have fun regularly. It's also important to save for and plan big events like travel, nice restaurants, and theater.

My personal issues here have always been an all or nothing approach. I either spend money that I shouldn't or I go long periods of time and don't do anything fun for myself or my family. This can be just as bad as overspending. Keeping money in a separate "fun" account is a great way to stay on track and know what your fun budget is.

If you use credit cards for points or cash back, just make sure the money is in your fun account to pay the card off at the end of the month. Using credit cards for points and extra stuff is fine if you are disciplined enough to do it right, otherwise the one percent that you receive from them is not worth the percentage that you have to pay them. Also remember that every credit card you own adds to your risk of identity theft.

5

Fluff in the Budget

I am constantly asked by people that are living on a tight budget if 30% of take home pay after tax is really enough to pay all the other bills? "Sure, your mom did it but that was a different time," they say. My response is always the same. "It sounds like we need to sit down and take a long hard look at your budget and see if we can find some places to cut costs."

Question #1: *How important is the car or cars?*
It's important to remember that most cars and trucks depreciate in value. They don't appreciate, which means that they are a tool not an investment. Too many people today buy a car for emotional not logical reasons. If you care for small children, need a car for your work, or live in an area without public transportation, then you need a reliable car. If not, chances are, you only own a car because you want a car. That's fine if your car payment, your insurance payment, the gas, and maintenance of the car take up no more than about 15% of your total budget. If your car or cars are costing you more than that, it's time to cut back or get a second job.

Question #2: *How important is your TV?*
I can't tell you the number of homes that I have gone into where I know that the people living in the house are struggling to make ends meet but they have some monster TV hooked up to cable or a satellite dish. And even better, that's usually not the only TV. Once again, television is a luxury, not a necessity. If your budget is tight it is one of the first places to cut back on for two reasons: #1 cost, #2 time consumption. Until you get your budget on track use your time for much wiser purposes than watching TV.

Question #3: *How much do you spend on tobacco and alcohol?*
No I'm not preaching to you. I love my beer, wine, and occasional cigar, but I don't spend more than 1% of my total budget on these things. If your budget is out of line, then it's time to cut back on or cut out tobacco and alcohol.

Question #4: *Is buying new really important to you and why?*
OK, I want new underwear, but aside from that, used usually works for me. Cars, appliances, furniture, clothing and so many other things that if we would simply buy used instead of new we could save thousands of dollars a year on. Garage sales are every where and many times just checking with friends to see if they know someone that's selling something you need is a great way to get good deals on stuff.

Question #5: *Is your cell phone more luxury than tool?*
If so, cut back on the luxury part. It's amazing to me when I think about my life without a cell phone and I realize that I can't seem to function without mine now and yet it was years before I got one. I must use my cell phone 10 times a day at least. My phone is simple, I don't text message or take pictures, I just talk on it. It's important to reevaluate your cell phone usage frequently and decide what functions you really need or what functions you just want and try to cut costs there. Also, always make your children responsible for paying for their own service. This will be a great lesson for them and a big budget saver for you.

Question #6: *Where do you get your groceries?*
Check out Angel Food Ministries. Joe and Linda Wingo founded Angel Food Ministries in 1994 to provide food for friends and neighbors who were struggling financially. Today, Angel Food Ministries is a non-profit, non-denominational organization dedicated to providing food relief to more than 500,000 families throughout the United States each month. In September 2008 for only $30 you would get, 1.5 lbs of Top Sirloin steak, 2 lbs pf boneless and skinless chicken breast, 3 lbs of breaded chicken chunks, 1.5 lbs of boneless pork filet, 20 oz. supreme pizza, 1lb ground turkey, 1lb cheddar cheese, bratwurst sausage, and an assortment of veggies, rice, beans, and other items. Go online to www.angelfoodministries.com[1] and get all the info. It will be worth your time.

During World War II our nation pulled together and everyone made sacrifices in order to achieve victory over the Nazis and the Japanese. We now refer to the people of that era as "The Greatest Generation" and we should. When Jimmy Carter was president he tried desperately to control oil prices by rationing gas purchases. He was not elected to a second term. Retired Senator Phil Graham recently gave a speech that accused the people of our nation of being whiners and not willing to make sacrifices in order to achieve our long term goals. The speech supposedly ended any chances that he may ever want to have in politics again. Unless we can change the way we think about what we want, need, and deserve, and find better ways to get the things we want without borrowing to get them, we as a nation are in serious trouble. We can learn from our parents and grandparents, it's time to start.

Home ownership and the American dream:
Bigger is not always better.

Sarah had gotten a promotion from her company, but with it came a transfer to a new town. No problem, the company was going to pay for her moving expenses and try to help her sell her old house. Ok, it all sounded easy enough but Sarah had some problems.

First of all, Sarah had bought the home that she lives in now at the peak of the housing market, so you guessed it, the home is worth slightly less than she owes on it. Then, the housing market that Sarah is moving into hasn't had the same downturn that Sarah's area has had, so she can't get the same size house for the same money. And finally, Sarah had run into a few minor credit problems since the purchase of her other home, so she was going to need more money for a down payment.

Emotionally, this is a very hard time for Sarah. She gets a pay raise and a promotion, and instead of getting a larger house, she has to get something smaller or rent a place to live. Emotionally, seems to be the key word here. What's wrong with taking a temporary step back in order to take a leap forward in the future?

Sarah should first look at the possibility of leasing her home now and see if it would offset rent payments in the new town. She should remember that other expenses will be involved with rent management and maintenance so she will need to get a bit more than she is paying on it or it is probably not a good option. Housing markets are cyclical like many other investments and often recover over time, so if she can wait to sell the house, she can probably recoup her investment.

The next step would be to take the loss on the house and simply buy a smaller house. She should pick the smallest house in the nicest neighborhood that she can afford. Her home should be a bit easier to sell that way once she can afford to upgrade to a bigger place, hopefully after making a profit on the smaller home.

As a last resort, Sarah should sell the home she has now and rent until her money and credit situation is better. She should try to find a place that costs no more than 15% of her monthly take home pay, saving the other 15% each month to buy a new home. Then she can decide how long she is willing to sacrifice in order to get the house she really wants.

If we take a step back from emotional issues and look at them from a logical standpoint, often we see that even the worst solution is better than sitting around and worrying about a problem. And as my grandfather and mother would tell you, a little sacrifice can go a long way towards getting what you want over time.

Investment Questions

I am often asked the question, "What is your IRA paying?" This question lets me know that the person asking the question needs to be educated on what an IRA is. An IRA is not an investment; it is a type of account that allows you to defer taxes, provided you qualify to have a traditional IRA account. The type of investment you pick in your IRA will determine the type of return you could receive. For example, if your IRA is invested in a CD with a 5% return, then you will receive 5%, as long as you wait until the CD matures. If it is invested in a different type of investment then you will not have a guaranteed return and your return will be based on the returns of the investments that you invest in. Some banks only have CDs as an investment option, which would add in causing the confusion among people that only invest their money with banks. IRAs have advantages and disadvantages that should be carefully discussed with your CPA and your CFP® or investment advisor before opening the account.

A Roth IRA is an account that allows you to invest money that you have paid taxes on already, but the gains and dividends on the money, once invested, grow tax deferred, and if you wait until you are 59 ½ years old to pull it out, then it comes out tax free. Both IRAs and Roth IRAs have special rules and penalties that must be discussed with your tax advisor before investing in one.

The next question I get is, "Annuities, are they good or bad?" My answer is always the same, "Yes." Annuities are a good fit for some portfolios, however, they are very complicated investments and the average investor has a hard time understanding exactly what it is and how much they are paying for it. Annuities have also been "pushed" on many unsuspecting investors by salesmen that have no real idea of the investors overall needs and goals. The bottom line is, if anyone talks to you about an annuity, and they don't clearly understand your personal situation, red flags should be going up. Don't buy an annuity until you have checked with your CPA and your CFP®. A really good CFP® or investment advisor will be happy to meet with your CPA and show them why the recommendation was made and where it fits into your portfolio, if it's a good fit.

I always love the question, "What is a penny stock and why is it so cheap?" My answer is, "they are cheap for a reason and they are something that you should stay away from." I have in the past had some investors that had the extra money and liked to gamble with it. That's fine, but I'm not a Vegas casino and I'm not someone that is going to help you with your gambling, so now that I am a CFP®, I want nothing to do with them.

"Are my investments FDIC insured?" If you have questions about your investments, you really need a financial advisor. Investment companies that don't use financial advisors are for people that clearly understand them, not for the beginner or novice investor. I equate it to hunting with a guide vs. hunting on your own. If you are going to hunt on your own; you need to know the territory, the gun, and what you're doing before you go.

And finally, my personal favorite: "Is the market going to go up, or down?" My answer: "Both." History tells us that over time markets recover, however no one can tell you with any real certainty what it will do in the near term. That is why I won't invest money that a client can't "tie up" for at least 2 years, usually longer. The last thing I want is for a client to call me and need money and I have to sell something at a loss in order to get it to them.

There are no dumb questions, but there are questions that show how uninformed a person is. If you are in the uninformed category, it's ok, accept it and start looking for an investment guide that can teach you how to hunt.

Notes

1. Raymond James Financial Services is not affiliated with and does not endorse Angel Food Ministries and is not responsible for their website content.

6

Purpose, Consistency, and Legacy

In May 2008 my mother and I took a trip to New Orleans. We were happy to see the progress that had taken place after hurricane Katrina. It was refreshing to see that the city was starting to bounce back. One afternoon, we decided to take a bus ride around the city and get off at some of the cemeteries. We started talking to the bus driver about the storm and the fact that the city seemed to be rebuilding so well. At that point, she told us her personal story, and it impressed me so much that I had to share it with you.

She said that she had stayed when the storm came in and like so many she had been trapped. Then after much hardship, they were finally rescued and sent to the Houston Astrodome. She had no access to money and was stuck in Houston for weeks, living in the Astrodome. But unlike many refugees from New Orleans, as soon as she had access to her funds and the means to get back to the city, she came back to rebuild her life. She had been making it on her own and she knew that she could do it again.

As soon as she could get her old bus driving job back, she did. She did most of the cleanup on her house herself. Most of all, she, in her own way was not only contributing to the rebuilding of her own life, but she was contributing to the rebuilding of New Orleans. Her purpose was clear, stand on her own feet; forget blame and anger, there was no time for that. Work consistently towards her goals and do her part to recreate the legacy that once was The City of New Orleans.

How many people never emotionally or financially recovered from that storm? How many times in your own life have you been distraught over some over bearing outside force that has brought you down and you thought that you would never recover from it? This woman did recover, and she was an inspiration to me and anyone that hears her story.

Cleo Whitlock was a World War II War hero. He was a fully recovered childhood victim of Polio. He was an inspiration and mentor to my cousin Russ and me. Russ used to say that, "No grey cats were allowed in Cleo's yard." What he meant was that with Cleo every thing was good or evil, there was no such thing as a grey area.

Cleo was big on accepting responsibility for mistakes and faults quickly so that you could get past them and move forward. He never passed the blame to someone else and he made sure that we, as his adopted sons, didn't either. His favorite saying was, "If you have a beating coming, raise your hand and be first in line to get yours out of the way, that way you're not sitting around worrying about it."

He believed in God, honesty, good morals, and good manners. When I knew him, Cleo's purpose in life was to be a good mentor to anyone that wanted his advice. His life itself was a consistent reminder of the caliber of person he was. He has left in me, Russ, his children and grandchildren a legacy of wisdom and simple honor that will never be forgotten.

In life we can learn so much from others. My friend Fred Kahl says, "Anyone you meet can have an impact on you if you let them. You can always learn something." He's right, I have learned what not to do from others as well as what to do. Each person I know, book I read, and experience I have leads me closer to who and what I can and should become if I am constantly searching for a better understanding of what true success means to me.

And finally, some of the best people I know are the ones that have suffered through the darkest valleys. They are the best money managers, because they went through a time when they had no money and rather than cry about it they went to work, saved, invested and fixed it. The toughest people are the ones that have experienced great pain and overcame it. And the most faithful are the ones that have dealt with the greatest hate and found a way to return it with great love. Embrace your hard times; they are what make you stronger.

In many corporations today, top executives get "golden parachutes" from the companies they run, which simply put means; they make big money even if the company fails. This teaches nothing. It is not the foundation of what this country was built on and is a stupid way to run a business. In life we should take responsibility for our action, that way we can learn something from our mistakes.

By now, you have probably figured out that "the simple way" is not necessarily the easy way. I also don't believe that I can change the world by writing a book. But I do believe that if enough people will start to search for their mission statement, develop a consistent path towards their goals and use some of the things they have learned in this book, then maybe when our grandchildren have children, our lives, this country, and the legacy that we have left for them will be something worth celebrating still.

God grant me the serenity to accept the things I can not change, the courage to change the things I can, and the wisdom to know the difference – Reinhold Niebuhr

Thank you for your time,

Jay Meador

About the Author

Jay is a native Texan and lives in College Station, Texas. He holds the Certified Financial Planner™ (CFP®) designation; a professional designation that requires a rigorous certification process as well as continuing education and development. He earned his bachelor's degree from Texas A & M University.

Using a hands-on approach to advising his clients, Jay takes the time to get to know each client and their unique predicaments. Based on individual factors such as personal goals, time horizon and tolerance for risk, he develops strategies designed to properly address his clients' diverse needs.

Jay may be contacted at any of the following:

(979) 693-7600
Jay.Meador@RaymondJames.com
www.raymondjames.com/jaymeador/

Raymond James Financial Service, Inc. is a FINRA and SIPC member

www.IsThereHopeForMe.com